The Promise Fulfilled

A Christmas Drama

David M. Allison

CSS Publishing Company, Inc.
Lima, Ohio

THE PROMISE FULFILLED

The Thompson Chain Reference® Bible, New International Version, copyright © 1983 by The B.B. Kirkbride Bible Company, Inc. and Zondervan Corporation, third printing, February 1984.

For more information about CSS Publishing Company resources, visit our website at www.csspub.com, email us at csr@csspub.com, or call (800) 241-4056.

e-book:
ISBN-13: 978-0-7880-2798-7
ISBN-10: 0-7880-2798-0

ISBN-13: 978-0-7880-2797-0
ISBN-10: 0-7880-2797-2   PRINTED IN USA

*I dedicate this book
to my wife Karla
and my son David.
They are a
blessing from God.*

Based on the gospel accounts given in Luke and Matthew, *The Promise Fulfilled* portrays a few of the marvelous events that surrounded the birth of our Lord and Savior Jesus Christ.

In seven scenes with six traditional songs, this play utilizes a multiple-character cast with a flexible number of extras.

Overview

Based on the gospel accounts given in Luke and Matthew, *The Promise Fulfilled* portrays a few of the marvelous events that surrounded the birth of our Lord and Savior Jesus Christ.

Scene 1: Aged saints Simeon and Anna, ever faithful to the promise that a Savior would come, head for the temple to see if the Messiah has arrived. Their friend, a Young Zealot — skeptical and impatient — has a run-in with a Roman Soldier.

Song: "O Come, O Come, Emmanuel"

Scene 2: The Virgin Mary is given the angelic announcement that she will bear the Child of Promise.

Scene 3: Joseph and Mary, on their way to Jerusalem to register for the census, search for a place to spend the night in Bethlehem.

Song: "Away In A Manger"

Scene 4: Shepherds round up their sheep and lie down to rest for the night. They are awakened by an angelic proclamation.

Song: "Angels From The Realms Of Glory"

Scene 5: Mary, Joseph, and the newborn baby Jesus receive some unexpected visitors: the three Magi and the joyful shepherds.

Song: "O Come, All Ye Faithful"

Scene 6: Mary and Joseph present baby Jesus to the Priest at the temple in Jerusalem. The Priest, Simeon, and Anna each praise God and bless the Child. The Young Zealot, seeing *The Promise Fulfilled* before his very eyes, turns from his violent ways and joins in the worship of the newborn King of Peace.

Song: "Joy To The World"

Closing Song: "Silent Night Holy Night"

[All songs: use audio recording, adult choir, cast as choir, or any combination]

SUGGESTED PROPS

Scene 1: canes, baby powder for "gray hair," "butter knife" dagger, Roman soldier: cape, sandals, helmet, long shorts, and red T-shirt

Scene 2: feather duster

Scene 3: manger, toy "baby Jesus," cloths, and blankets

Scene 4: canes or staffs for shepherd's crooks, cardboard sheep

Scene 5: crowns; items for gold, frankincense, and myrrh; shepherd crooks

Scene 6: baptismal font, "butter knife" dagger, white robe for priest

SPECIAL NOTES

The play is flexible. You can use as many extras as you like by adding shepherds, Magi entourage, people milling about near the inns, and the like. You will also need some stagehands for scene and prop changes.

You can get elaborate with the sets, robes, props, or do it so simply that it is done on a "shoestring" budget. The glory is in the biblical story.

If you have younger children you may hide copies of the play in the props. If they need it, they can get to their lines and read them. Also, teach them to "just roll with it" or "incorporate it" if someone makes a mistake. Some of the best memories and enjoyment by the audience is experienced when someone does something "cute" but technically "wrong." Teach them that the audience is "for" them. Help them to *embrace* the audience looking on. People want them to do well and are very forgiving if they don't let on.

The line by the Priest on page 27 translates: "Peace God. Jesus the Messiah." It adds a touch of Jewish cultural depth by way of a few Hebrew words in basic form.

Pray and ask God to bless your performance of this play for his glory.

CHARACTERS

Simeon, the aged prophet
Anna, the aged prophetess
Young Zealot
Roman Soldier
Roman Soldier Extras
Mary, the mother of Jesus
Joseph, the husband of Mary
Shepherd #1
Shepherd #2
Shepherd Extras
Magi #1
Magi #2
Magi #3
Innkeeper #1
Innkeeper #2
Innkeeper #3
Priest
Narrator

Scene 1

The Faith of Simeon and Anna

(Luke 2:25-27, 36-37. Scene 1 cast begins to the rear in a sanctuary or offstage. Overhead light is on. Other lights are very dim. A stanza of "O Come, O Come, Emmanuel" is playing softly. As the music stops, the narrator begins.)

Narrator: Christmas is a time of hope and joy. People of every age wait expectantly. They wait "forward," for Christmas morning when they can finally open their presents. The waiting is what makes it fun but it is also the hardest part. Christmas can seem like it will never come!

Journey back in time with us, to ancient Israel in the days before the Messiah had come. Abraham's descendants had grown into a nation and had endured the slavery in Egypt, the exodus, the attacks of the Philistines, and even a time of captivity in Babylon. Now they were suffering under the mighty Roman empire and her occupation armies.

Old Testament prophets had long predicted a Messiah would come; an Anointed One who would break the power that held them in bondage. Many waited expectantly for the coming Messiah. They waited "forward." Yet others began to lose hope in the promise. They sought to expel the Romans by force. These zealots would spare no opportunity to show the Romans just what they thought of them.

Luke's gospel tells of two who waited "forward" for the coming Messiah: Simeon and Anna. *"Now there was a man in Jerusalem called Simeon, who was righteous and devout. He was waiting for the consolation of Israel, and the Holy Spirit was upon him. It had been revealed to him by the Holy Spirit that he would not die before he had seen the Lord's Christ. Moved by the Spirit, he went into the temple courts... There was also a prophetess, Anna... She was very old... She never left the temple but worshiped night and day, fasting and praying."*

Let's watch now as Simeon and Anna make their way to the temple expecting the Messiah to come any day. An impatient-but-friendly Young Zealot follows after them.

(Spotlight comes on. Simeon and Anna, on canes, with baby-powdered gray hair, head toward the front. Young Zealot follows just behind, calls to them, and catches up.)

Young Zealot: Hey Simeon! Anna! Wait up!

Anna: You shouldn't have much trouble catching *us*!

Young Zealot: Hey! Where are you going?

Simeon: Son, you *know* where we're going! To the temple! We don't want to keep the young Messiah waiting now, do we?

Young Zealot: Don't you ever get sick of going up there and wasting all your time? The Messiah wasn't there yesterday and he won't be there *today* either! And even if he was, what are we gonna do? Wait 25 years, while he grows up, before we fight these Romans?

Anna: Son, you have faith in your *own* might, but you don't seem to have any faith in *God*! Don't you believe the scripture?

Young Zealot: Yeah, I guess I do. But *(revealing and flashing a butter knife dagger)* I also think God helps those who help themselves! And it's gonna take a lot more than going to the temple to get rid of all these pork-eating Romans!

Roman Soldier: *(in a hurry — barging through)* Out of the way, you Hebrew pig! I'm going to be late!

Young Zealot: Pig? You've got a lotta nerve, you pagan! *(makes spitting motion and sound)*

Roman Soldier: That's it! You're mine now, sonny boy! Let's see how you like the whipping post! *(Roman Soldier drags him away.)*

(Simeon and Anna tug at the soldier's arms to no avail.)

Anna: *(turns to Simeon)* I know how the boy feels, but he has so little faith. I'm going to pray they let him go.

Simeon: Yes, Anna. Let's do that! As soon as we get to the temple! I can't wait to see if the Messiah is here anyway. Come on, let's go! *(stage goes dark, then overhead lights come on)*

SONG: "O Come, O Come, Emmanuel"

Scene 2

Mary's Song

(Luke 1:26-38, overhead light only as Mary makes her way center stage.)

Narrator: Simeon, Anna, the Young Zealot — indeed — all the people of Israel were waiting for the promised Messiah. Little did they know that he was about to come onto the stage of world history to change hearts and lives forever! Just nine months earlier a very humble, pure, young woman was informed she would be honored above all women who would ever live. She would bear the Christ Child! Let's watch as she learns the wonderful news.

Mary: *(momentary pause as Mary busies herself with light housework)*

Narrator: "In the sixth month, God sent the angel Gabriel to Nazareth, a town in Galilee, to a virgin pledged to be married to a man named Joseph, a descendant of David. The virgin's name was Mary. The angel went to her and said… *(Spotlight comes on from the rear, then the reading continues.)* 'Greetings, you who are highly favored! The Lord is with you.' Mary was greatly troubled at his words and wondered what kind of greeting this might be. But the angel said to her, 'Do not be afraid, Mary, you have found favor with God. You will be with child and give birth to a son, and you are to give him the name Jesus. He will be great and will be called the Son of the Most High. The Lord will give him the throne of his father David, and he will reign over the house of Jacob forever; his kingdom will never end.'"

Mary: How will this be, since I am a virgin?

Narrator: The angel answered, "The Holy Spirit will come upon you, and the power of the Most High will overshadow you. So the holy one to be born will be called the Son of God... nothing is impossible with God."

Mary: *(gets down on her knees and puts her hands together as if to pray)* I am the Lord's servant. May it be to me as you have said. *(Mary bows her head as lights go out. No song for this scene.)*

Scene 3

No Room

(Luke 2:1-7)

Narrator: "In those days Caesar Augustus issued a decree that a census should be taken of the entire Roman world... And everyone went to his own town to register. So Joseph also went up from the town of Nazareth in Galilee to Judea, to Bethlehem the town of David, because he belonged to the house and line of David. He went there to register with Mary, who was pledged to be married to him and was expecting a child. While they were there, the time came for the baby to be born... there was no room for them in the inn."

(Mary and Joseph make their way to the front — lights are dim.)

Joseph: *(turning to Mary)* It's getting late Mary and the town is so crowded. I hope we can find a place to stay. Wait here and I'll see if anyone has room.

*(Joseph goes to two "inn" doors asking if they have room. Both times the innkeeper **rudely** dismisses him by making a face, shaking his head "no," and then slamming the door. Joseph then begs the third innkeeper.)*

Could we just stay in your barn? With the animals? Please! My wife is going to have a *baby*!

(Smiling, Joseph leads Mary up to center stage where she lays down on some blankets. Joseph kneels beside her and holds her hand. Lights go out.)

(Stage hands provide a toy baby in cloths. Lights come back up with Mary now holding the baby Jesus. Joseph looks on.)

Narrator: "And she gave birth to her firstborn, a son. She wrapped him cloths and placed him in a manger."

Mary: *(placing the baby in the manger)* Goodnight Jesus.

(lights out)

SONG: "Away In A Manger"

Scene 4

Shepherd Scene

(Luke 2:8-20, overhead light on)

Narrator: "And there were shepherds living out in the fields nearby, keeping watch over their flocks at night."

(Lights dim, shepherds "round up sheep" and, yawning, lay down to sleep.)

Shepherd #1: *(pointing outward)* Is that a new star up there?

Shepherd #2: I think it is! Look, it's getting closer! And brighter!

(rear spotlight on — shepherds draw back in terror)

Narrator: "An angel of the Lord appeared to them, and the glory of the Lord shone around them, and they were terrified. But the angel said to them, 'Do not be afraid. I bring you good news of great joy that will be for all the people. This will be a sign to you: You will find a baby wrapped in cloths and lying in a manger.' "

(light from rear becomes brighter)

Narrator: "Suddenly a great company of heavenly host appeared with the angel, praising God and saying, 'Glory to God in the highest, and on earth peace to men on whom his favor rests.' "

(lights back to dim suddenly; overhead light only)

Shepherd #1: Let's go back to Bethlehem and check this out! I can't believe God sent angels to tell us about it! This is big!

Shepherd #2: This is *really* big!

(all shepherds run off to see the baby Jesus)

SONG: "Angels From The Realms Of Glory"

Scene 5

Visit of the Magi

(Lights are dim and come up slightly as Mary and Joseph look at baby Jesus in the manger. The Magi knock loudly.)

Joseph: *(answering the door)* Can I help you? *(Three Magi enter slowly. Stunned, Joseph backs toward Mary.)* Who are you?

Magi #1: *(disregarding Joseph's question)* Is this the one who has been born King of the Jews?

Magi #2: *(excited after traveling to see him)* We saw his star, in the East!

Magi #3: We have come... to worship him.

(Joseph and Mary look at each other in amazement. The Magi bow down, faces to the ground, hands extended in worship. Then, still on their knees.)

Magi #1: We have gifts for him: Gold! *(places gold by the manger)*

Magi #2: Frankincense! *(places frankincense by the manger)*

Magi #3: And myrrh! *(places myrrh by the manger)*

(Another knock is heard — Joseph waves the shepherds in.)

Shepherd #1: Look! There's the baby, in a manger, just like the angel said!

(Shepherds come closer and kneel. Magi bow again in worship. Mary and Joseph bow their heads as if to pray.)

(lights out and back on for song)

SONG: "O Come, All Ye Faithful"

Scene 6

Jesus Presented at the Temple

(Luke 2:21-40; Numbers 6:24-26)

Narrator: As we have seen, some glorious events had taken place in those months and days; events that neither Simeon, Anna, nor the Young Zealot could have known about. Let's return to Jerusalem now, as Simeon and Anna are entering the temple.

(Mary and Joseph walk in slowly from the side, while Simeon and Anna come down the center. A Priest is waiting at center stage by a baptismal font. All walk slowly as the narrator reads. When they reach the center, they wait. Young Zealot works his way to the center last, without drawing attention.)

Narrator: "On the eighth day, when it was time to circumcise him, he was named Jesus, the name angel had given him before he had been conceived. When the time of their purification according to the Law of Moses had been completed, Joseph and Mary took him to Jerusalem to present him to the Lord."

(Mary hands Jesus to the priest who raises him up.)

Priest: Shalom Jehovah! *Yeshua ha Mashiach.*[1] *(Priest bows his head.)*

Simeon: *(to Joseph and Mary)* I've waited so long, may I hold him?

Joseph: Yes, our friend, you may! *(Priest hands Jesus to Simeon.)*

Simeon: *(lifting the baby heavenward)* Lord, you have kept your promise! You now dismiss your servant in peace! My eyes have seen your salvation! Blessed be the name of the Lord! *(hands Jesus back to Mary)*

Anna: *(lifting her hands toward heaven)* Thanks be to God, who hears the cries of his people! May his name be praised forever! He has shown us the Anointed One!

(Priest raises his hands toward heaven as Mary and Joseph kneel. Young Zealot throws down his dagger and kneels. Simeon places his hands on Joseph and Mary's heads. Anna places her hands on their backs.)

Simeon: Unto you a child is born, unto us a Savior is given. The Lord bless you and keep you. The Lord make his face to shine upon you and give you peace. Amen.

(All stand and embrace as lights dim and go out briefly then back on for song.)

SONG: "Joy To The World"

---

1. Pronunciation: YE - SHOE - A HA MA - SHEE - OCK

Scene 7

How About You?

(Dim light, Scene 6 characters stay. The rest of the cast joins a few at a time, greets them silently, and take turns peaking at the baby Jesus.)

Narrator: How about you? Is there room for Jesus in *your* heart? Have you invited him in to be *your* Lord and Savior? This Christmas, as we celebrate Jesus' *first* coming, let's not forget that he is coming *again*. Are you prepared to meet him? He came that you might be cleansed and forgiven of your sins. Please, open your heart and make room for Jesus! That will truly give you a Merry Christmas!

(Lights go out completely. Then one at a time cast members light and lift candles.)

SONG: "Silent Night"

(At the end of the song, Joseph counts aloud but quietly "1, 2, 3" for timing.)

ENTIRE CAST: Merry Christmas!

www.ingramcontent.com/pod-product-compliance
Lightning Source LLC
Chambersburg PA
CBHW071808020426
42331CB00008B/2437